ET READY FOR A BLAST OF WEB-TASTIC ACTION,
URTESY OF YOUR FRIENDLY NEIGHBOURHOOD...

SPIDER-MAN ®™

CONTENTS

£6.99

THE MAKING OF A... SPIDER-MAN®™

EARLY DAYS...

Orphaned at a young age, Peter Parker was raised like a son by his Aunt May and Uncle Ben. However, being a shy but intelligent child, Peter had trouble making friends at school.

A SPIDER'S FATE!

His life changed forever the day he attended a lecture on a new experimental type of radiation. A harmless spider wandered into the scientific machinery and received an amazing jolt of *radiation*. Near death and in shock, the seemingly insignificant arachnid crawled from the device and **bit Peter Parker!**

EXTRAORDINARY POWERS!

Slowly Peter realised that the bite had made him *stronger, faster* and more *agile*. Realising he could use his new abilities to make money for his aunt and uncle, he became an amateur wrestler!

WALKING AWAY...

One night after a wrestling match, a burglar broke into the stadium office and stole all the money from the safe. As the felon ran from the building he encountered Peter Parker. Although he could have stopped the criminal using his new powers, Peter decided it was someone else's problem and did nothing.

TRAGEDY!

Returning to his home a couple of hours later, Peter made a terrible discovery. His beloved Uncle Ben had been shot and killed by an intruder! Wearing his makeshift wrestling outfit, Peter set off in pursuit of his uncle's murderer.

THE HARDEST LESSON..

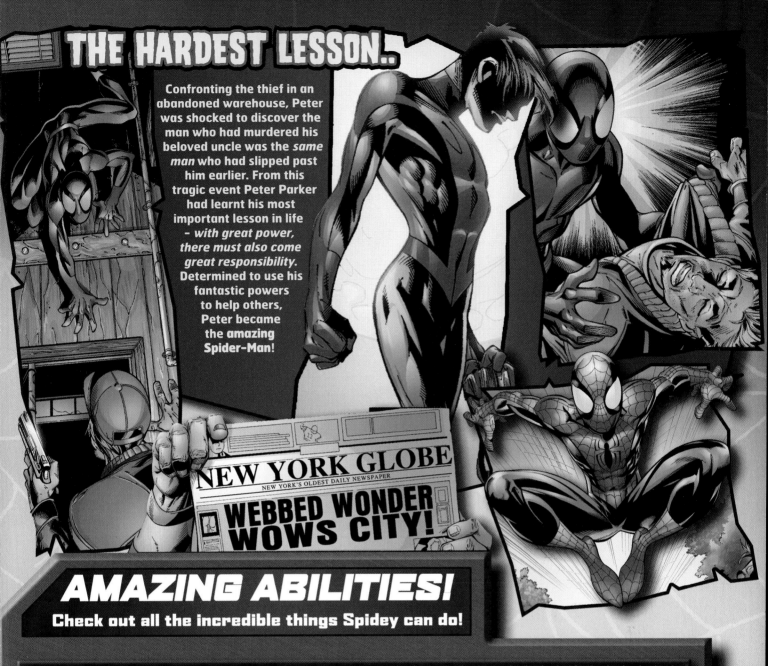

Confronting the thief in an abandoned warehouse, Peter was shocked to discover the man who had murdered his beloved uncle was the *same man* who had slipped past him earlier. From this tragic event Peter Parker had learnt his most important lesson in life – *with great power, there must also come great responsibility.* Determined to use his fantastic powers to help others, Peter became the amazing Spider-Man!

NEW YORK GLOBE
NEW YORK'S OLDEST DAILY NEWSPAPER
WEBBED WONDER WOWS CITY!

AMAZING ABILITIES!
Check out all the incredible things Spidey can do!

Just like a real spider, he can defy gravity and cling to any surface!

Spidey can lift over 25 tons!

Peter designed two special 'web-slingers' that attach to his wrists. By tapping his palm with his fingers, he can fire a length of sticky webbing to swing from buildings or ensnare his foes.

One of the most useful abilities Peter gained from the spider's bite is his spider-sense! This amazing power can warn Spidey of any danger nearby!

AMAZING ABILITIES!

Could Spider-Man be outmatched? He has certainly never met a villain quite as fearsome, quite as determined, or quite as...**bald** as the Vulture!

Unless, of course, you count the last time they fought...

THE RETURN OF THE VULTURE!

STAN LEE & STEVE DITKO   DANIEL QUANTZ   JONBOY MEYERS   PAT DAVIDSON   UDON'S LARRY MOLINAR   ERIK KO   VC'S RANDY GENTILE
PLOT   SCRIPT   PENCILS   INKS   COLORS   UDON CHIEF   LETTERER

MACKENZIE CADENHEAD & NICK LOWE   C.B. CEBULSKI   RALPH MACCHIO   JOE QUESADA   DAN BUCKLEY
ASSISTANT EDITORS   EDITOR   CONSULTING EDITOR   EDITOR-IN-CHIEF   PUBLISHER

It was an epic battle high above the New York City streets!

The Vulture had been robbing the city blind, until Spider-Man deduced his secret of flight: A unique form of magnetic power!

So, Spider-Man created a powerful magnetic inverter, which he used against the Vulture in their final battle.

No longer able to fly, the Vulture was grounded where the police were waiting to put him in jail.

You haven't seen the last of me, Spider-Man!

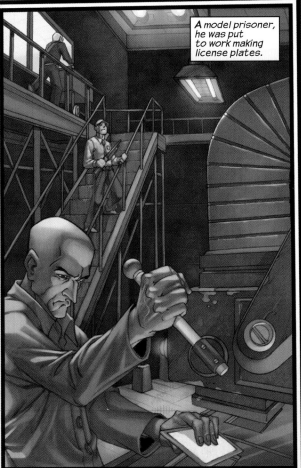

A model prisoner, he was put to work making license plates.

But right under their noses, he stole parts to make a brand new flying device!

Fools.

3782-454

CONTINUED ON PAGE 16

13

THE VULTURE!

EVIL ORIGINS

REACH FOR THE SKIES!
Adrian Toomes was a successful businessman who dreamed of one day creating an electro-magnetic harness that would enable a man to fly.

BETRAYED!
His life of crime began when his unscrupulous partner took over their company and fired him. Enraged by what had happened, Toomes stole his prototype harness and swore revenge on his former friend.

THE WINGS OF REVENGE!
Using his flying harness, Toomes broke into his old company and robbed them blind. Intoxicated by his new found sense of power, he decided to embark upon a citywide crime spree and renamed himself the Vulture!

SPIDEY DATA FILE #1

As cruel and cunning as the flying scavenger he takes his name from, the Vulture has been a thorn in Spidey's side since the very beginning of his crime-fighting career!

ADRIAN TOOMES

>>DATA:3459 542/7

VULT 291

CODE 435 ZV6

Occupation: Professional Criminal

STRENGTH	3
AGILITY	4
INTELLIGENCE	4
FIGHTING SKILLS	2

Powers / Abilities: On top of his natural cunning, the Vulture uses a special electro-magnetic harness that gives him the power to fly!

SLICE N' DICE!

His wings are tipped with razor sharp edges to slice and dice anyone foolish enough to get close to him.

POWER BOOST!

He might look like a weak old man but the Vulture is actually one of Spidey's most agile foes! His natural athletic abilities are boosted to incredible levels by the electro-magnetic waves from his harness!

AMAZING CONTROL!

Due to his amazing agility, the Vulture can fly through even the tightest corridors!

BIRD-BRAINED!

Even without his harness, the Vulture would still be a great threat thanks to his high intelligence and natural cunning!

HIGH FLYER!

The Vulture can fly at speeds of up to 95mph and can reach an altitude of 11500 feet.

15

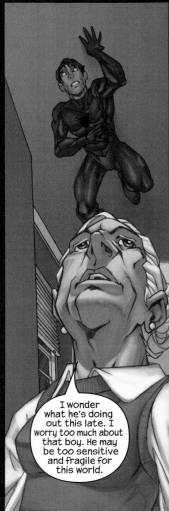

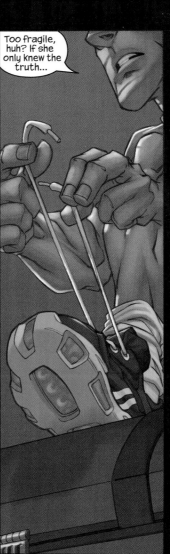

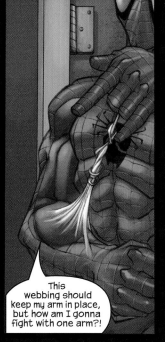

CONTINUED ON PAGE 28

ULTIMATE BATTLE!

Being the world's most famous web-slinger is no easy job! Over the years I've had to battle some of the most dangerous villains in the entire universe! Check out this round up of my top 5 toughest battles!

SPIDER-MAN

1

VS THE HULK

On a number of occasions Spidey has been forced to go toe-to-toe with the jolly green giant! Although Spidey has never been strong enough to take the Hulk down, his spider-sense and natural agility make it nearly impossible for ol' green skin to lay a finger on him!

VS

2

If you thought Venom was dangerous, you ain't seen nothing yet! Like Venom, Carnage is an alien symbiote but his host is a totally psychotic serial killer called Cletus Kasady. As Carnage could neutralize Spidey's spider-sense and knew all his secrets, defeating him was nearly impossible. He eventually had to team-up with none other than Venom to take down the slimy red scumbag!

Carnage

3 **VS**

Thanks to the powers of the Ruby Crystal of Cytorrak, the Juggernaut is completely unstoppable! He could easily shrug off anything Spidey threw at him, including a tanker truck full of gasoline! Spidey realised that he could not defeat him with might, so he lead the Juggernaut into the recently poured foundations of a nearby building. As the concrete set, the unstoppable villain found himself permanently entombed!

THE JUGGERNAUT

VS

4

The Sinister Six are a super villain team made up of Spidey's very worst foes! Led by Dr. Octopus, the gang kidnapped Betty Brant and Aunt May, and challenged Spider-Man to rescue them. One after another, he was forced to fight all of the unruly bunch. By the time he reached Dr. Octopus, Spidey was completely exhausted but with his last ounces of strength he was able to defeat Doc Ock and rescue Betty and his beloved aunt.

The Sinister Six

5 **VS**

COSMIC SPIDEY

The Tri-Sentinel was made from three mutant hunting robots that were merged together by the trickster god Loki. The robot was almost unstoppable, highly intelligent and had a vast array of weapons at its disposal! Luckily, a few weeks before Spidey had received a jolt of cosmic energy that had boosted his powers to even more amazing levels. The two battled long and hard, and Spidey eventually destroyed him by using the last of the cosmic energy left in his body!

THE TRI-SENTINEL!

SPIDEY'S WEB OF PUZZLES!

Hey, web heads! I've got my hands full at the moment taking on the Vulture and the Sandman, but there's still a whole host of villains in New York who need teaching a lesson! Can you guys help me catch some of the other crooks by solving the puzzles below?

SUPER VILLAIN SHOWDOWN!

Uh-oh! Nearly all of the webbed wonder's foes have teamed up to try and take him down! Help Spidey beat them all by spotting their names in the word grid below!

WHAT IS THIS? A MEETING FOR FREAKS ANONYMOUS?!

```
N   O R T C E L E T   A
C U Y A R M Y S T E R I O A O V
A K E R V B G T M G I V V
R E E I M A K R R H I N O
N K L Z O S A C B C I K
A C R D N P A E O L E I V
G A B A E O M N B L J N U
E E U D V L B O D O R G L
A L J C K E G A O M O P T
A U S I B N N U S A I U R
  J A C K O L A N T E R N R
  U A S H O C K E R E R E N E
      R G E E
```

SANDMAN
ELECTRO   KRAVEN
KINGPIN   SHOCKER
VULTURE   RHINO
HOBGOBLIN

MYSTERIO
CARNAGE   VENOM
JACK O'LANTERN

MULTIPLE MENACE!

The Green Goblin has created six robotic clones to fool and confuse Spider-Man! Take a look and see if you can spy which one is the real deal!

A   B   C

ORIGINAL

D   E   F

End. 33

A STING IN THE TALE!

RULES

The Scorpion has stolen a small fortune in money and jewels and it's up to New York's greatest Super Heroes to get it back!

Here's your chance to stop one of Spidey's most vicious villains and save the day!

You will need:

A Dice
4 Counters (You can use the counters printed on page 62, or if you don't want to cut-up your annual, you can photocopy the page or use 4 coins or buttons.)

How To Play:

This is a game for 2 to 4 players. Each player picks a counter (Either Spider-Man, Daredevil, Luke Cage or Spider-Woman) and then rolls the dice. The person with the highest score moves first, then the person on his left and so on.

As you move round the board, you must follow the instructions on each of the squares. If you land on a red square, you need to battle one of Spidey's enemies! On your next go, roll the dice and try to beat the score shown. If you do not beat it, you must stay on that square till your next go and try again. If you roll higher, then you can roll the dice again and move on that many number of squares.

The first person to reach the Scorpion is the winner! Good luck!

OKAY, SPIDER-FANS! LET'S SEND THE GREEN-SKINNED GOON BACK TO THE SLAMMER!

17

TRICKED BY MYSTERIO, GO BACK 4 SPACES!

START

2

2+
BLACK CAT!

15

ATTACKED BY THE SINISTER SIX! RETURN TO START!

13

CHAMELEON!
3+

4

5

10   11

3+
BULLSEYE!

7   8   9

STOP TO HELP AUNT

18

20

21

ELECTRO! 3+

DR. DOOM! 5+

27

26

25

23

THE HULK! 5+

29 THE AVENGERS OFFER YOU A LIFT! ROLL AND MOVE TWICE NEXT TURN!

24 THE THING SMASHES YOU A SHORT CUT!

30

31 HELP FROM IRON MAN! GO FORWARD 3 SQUARES!

32

33 ATTACKED BY SPIDER-SLAYERS! BACK 5 SQUARES!

34

35

DR. OCTOPUS! 5+

39

38

THE LIZARD! 3+

36

41

43 SAVE A BABY FROM A BURNING BUILDING! MISS A TURN!

44

46

47

42

CARNAGE! 6+

FINISH

TO STOP THE SANDMAN!

STAN LEE & STEVE DITKO   **DANIEL QUANTZ**   **JONBOY MEYERS**   **PAT DAVIDSON**   **UDON'S LARRY MOLINAR**   **ERIK KO**   **VC'S RANDY GENTILE**
PLOT   SCRIPT   PENCILS   INKS   C O L O R S   UDON CHIEF   L E T T E R E R

MACKENZIE CADENHEAD & NICK LOWE   **C.B. CEBULSKI**   **RALPH MACCHIO**   **JOE QUESADA**   **DAN BUCKLEY**
ASSISTANT EDITORS   EDITOR   CONSULTING EDITOR   EDITOR-IN-CHIEF   P U B L I S H E R

CONTINUED ON PAGE 44

THE SANDMAN!

EVIL ORIGINS

BAD TO THE BONE!

Flint Marko had spent his whole life on the wrong side of the law. After a string of high-profile robberies he was finally caught and sent to a maximum security prison. However, one night he managed to escape through an unguarded drainage tunnel.

ON THE RUN!

Becoming one of the most wanted men in America, Flint hid in the one place he thought nobody would look for him, an atomic weapons testing site! Marko believed the site was no longer in use but he was proved wrong the day he was caught in the blast of a nuclear test explosion!

EVERY GRAIN OF SAND...

Incredibly, the radioactive explosion caused his body to fuse with the sand around him, making him virtually indestructible! With his new found powers, the Sandman returned to his former life of crime and became one of New York's most deadly felons!

SPIDEY DATA FILE #2

Getting sand in his eyes is the least of Spidey's worries when he has to tangle with this granular goon! Read on to discover how a two-bit criminal became one of the webbed wonder's most dangerous foes!

FLINT MARKO

>>>DATA:3349 545/9

SAND 337

CODE 555 ZX1

Occupation: Professional Criminal

STRENGTH	5
AGILITY	3
INTELLIGENCE	2
FIGHTING SKILLS	3

Powers / Abilities: Instead of normal flesh and bone, his body is made up entirely of sand which he can manipulate in a variety of ways.

SHAPE-SHIFTER!

He can shift his body into any shape imaginable, giving him an almost limitless reach with his rock hard fists!

He can try to suffocate his opponents by dispersing the sand in his body and surrounding them!

ULTIMATE POWER!

The Sandman can alter the density of his body so that it can flow like water or become as hard as steel!

STRONG MAN!

The Sandman is strong enough to lift over 80 tons!

TAKE A SHOWER!

Although he may seem indestructible, the Sandman's one big weakness is water! If he gets a good soaking the fragmented felon turns into an unwieldy mud-monster and loses all his natural agility.

CONTINUED FROM PAGE 41

Parker Residence.

WHY COULDN'T I HAVE CHOSEN A SIMPLE COSTUME THAT'D BE EASY TO REPAIR? LIKE REALLY COOL SUNGLASSES AND A LEATHER JACKET OR SOMETHING.

I GUESS WE CAN RULE SEWING OUT AS ONE OF MY SUPERPOWERS.

OUCH! HOW DOES AUNT MAY DO IT? WISH I COULD ASK HER TO STITCH UP MY MASK WITHOUT MAKING HER SUSPI-- HEY! WHAT'S THIS??

"TWO MONTHS AGO, THE SO-CALLED SANDMAN WAS JUST A MAN-- AN INCARCERATED MAN."

"KNOWN THEN AS FLINT MARKO, HE WAS ONE OF THE MOST NOTORIOUS INMATES IN NEVADA'S MAXIMUM-SECURITY SAN MIGUEL PRISON."

"HIS SENTENCE WAS NATURAL LIFE FOR ASSAULT AND ARMED ROBBERY. HIS PROSPECTS FOR PAROLE WERE SLIM, AT BEST. THAT IS, UNTIL HE AND TWO OTHERS ORCHESTRATED A DARING JAILBREAK."

"THOUGH POLICE APPREHENDED THE OTHERS, MARKO MANAGED TO ESCAPE."

"HE REMAINED AT LARGE AND EVADED POLICE BY HIDING OUT IN THE ONE PLACE NO ONE THOUGHT HE'D BE DUMB ENOUGH TO GO..."

UNITED STATES MILITARY NUCLEAR TEST AREA **NO TRESPASSING**

"THE AIR FORCE BOMBING RANGE. THOUGH MARKO MANAGED TO STAY OUT OF HARM'S WAY AT FIRST, HIS LUCK RAN OUT WHEN THE GOVERNMENT BEGAN TESTING A NEW SERIES OF TACTICAL NUCLEAR WEAPONS."

HEY! WHAT'S THIS GOOPY STUFF ON MY CHAIR?! IT'S STICKING MY ARM TO THE--

I'M STUCK! IS THIS SOMEONE'S IDEA OF A JOKE?! POURING GLUE ON MY CHAIR?!!

SIR, IT LOOKS LIKE IT COULD POSSIBLY BE... WEBBING.

HI, PETER! COME BY TO SEE ME?

ACTUALLY, I NEED TO SEE MR. JAMESON, BUT SEEING YOU SURE IS A NICE BONUS.

THEN HERE, GIVE THESE PANTS TO HIM WHILE YOU'RE IN THERE.

SURE THING, MS. BRANT!

YOU. LISTEN, KID, IF YOU'RE NOT CARRYING PICTURES OF SPIDER-MAN ROBBING A BANK, THEN I DON'T WANT TO SEE YOU RIGHT NOW.

NO, BUT I AM CARRYING YOUR SLACKS.

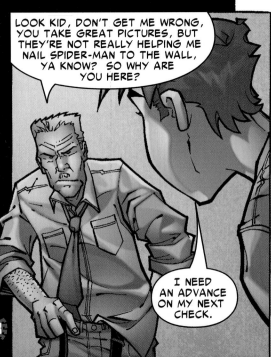

LOOK KID, DON'T GET ME WRONG, YOU TAKE GREAT PICTURES, BUT THEY'RE NOT REALLY HELPING ME NAIL SPIDER-MAN TO THE WALL, YA KNOW? SO WHY ARE YOU HERE?

I NEED AN ADVANCE ON MY NEXT CHECK.

WHAT HAPPENED TO YOU?

DON'T ASK.

DID I HEAR YOU RIGHT, LIZ? YOU'RE GOING ON A DATE WITH PUNY PETER PARKER TONIGHT?

WELL, YEAH, FLASH. PETER'S BEEN ASKING SO MANY TIMES, I JUST DIDN'T HAVE THE HEART TO TURN HIM DOWN *AGAIN*.

I needed that money for some new experiments with my webbing... Hey! If I can defeat the Sandman *TONIGHT* and take pictures, I could win the city over *AND* get the money I need from Jameson!

SO, WHAT TIME ARE YOU PICKING ME UP TONIGHT, PETER?

WHAT? TONIGHT?! I TOTALLY--

FORGOT?

NO! I, UH, I JUST, I CAN'T... I NEED TO STUDY FOR A TEST--

HE ALREADY HAS A DATE TONIGHT, LIZ-- WITH THE LOVELY ALGEBERELLA!

STRAIGHT-A STUDENT AND YOU CAN'T TAKE A NIGHT OFF FOR A DATE?! I FEEL SORRY FOR YOU, PETER.

ME TOO.

PETER! JUST THE BOY I WANTED TO SEE. I NEED YOU TO BRING SOME LAB EQUIPMENT DOWN TO THE BASEMENT.

SURE THING, MR. MILLER. IT'S NOT LIKE I'VE GOT ANYTHING BETTER TO DO-- LIKE WIN THE GIRL BACK.

CONTINUED ON PAGE 54

CONTINUED ON PAGE 54

51

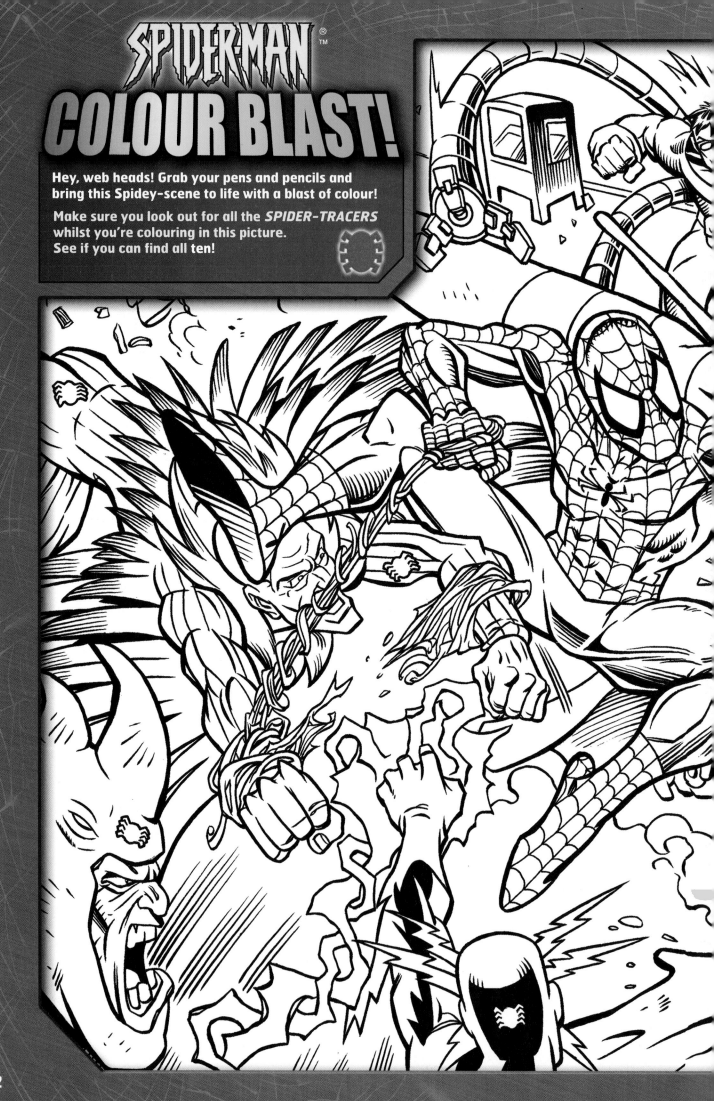

SPIDER-MAN ®™
COLOUR BLAST!

Hey, web heads! Grab your pens and pencils and bring this Spidey-scene to life with a blast of colour!

Make sure you look out for all the **SPIDER-TRACERS** whilst you're colouring in this picture.
See if you can find all ten!

57

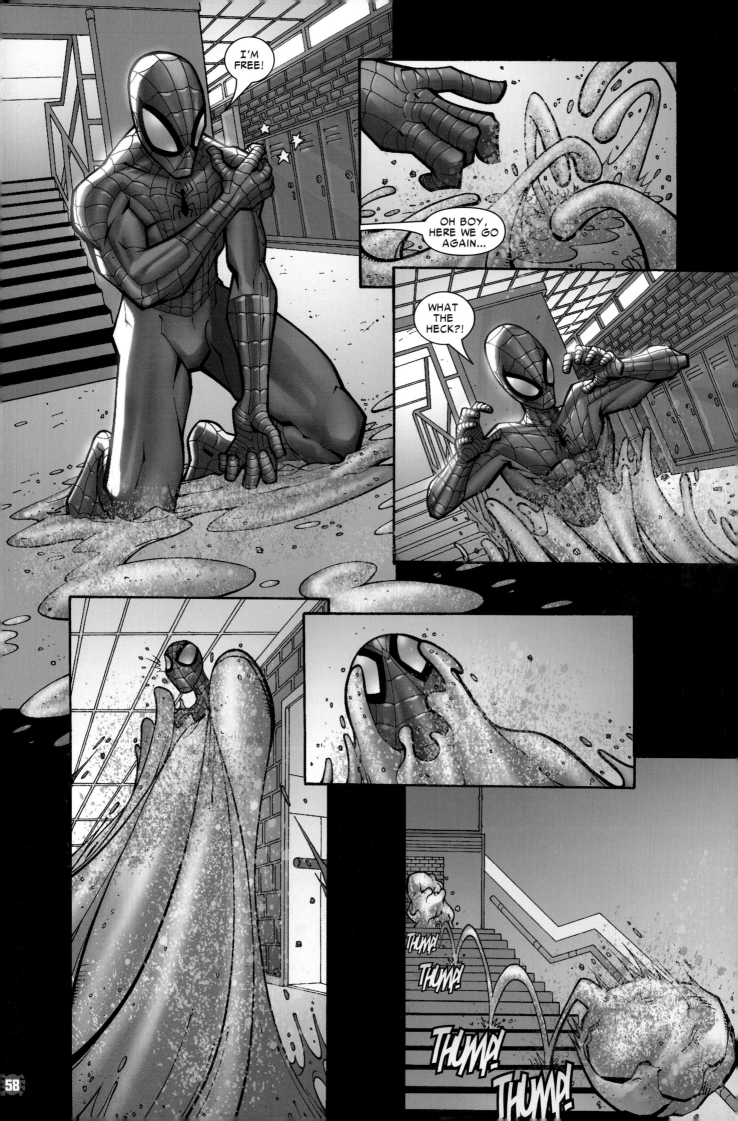

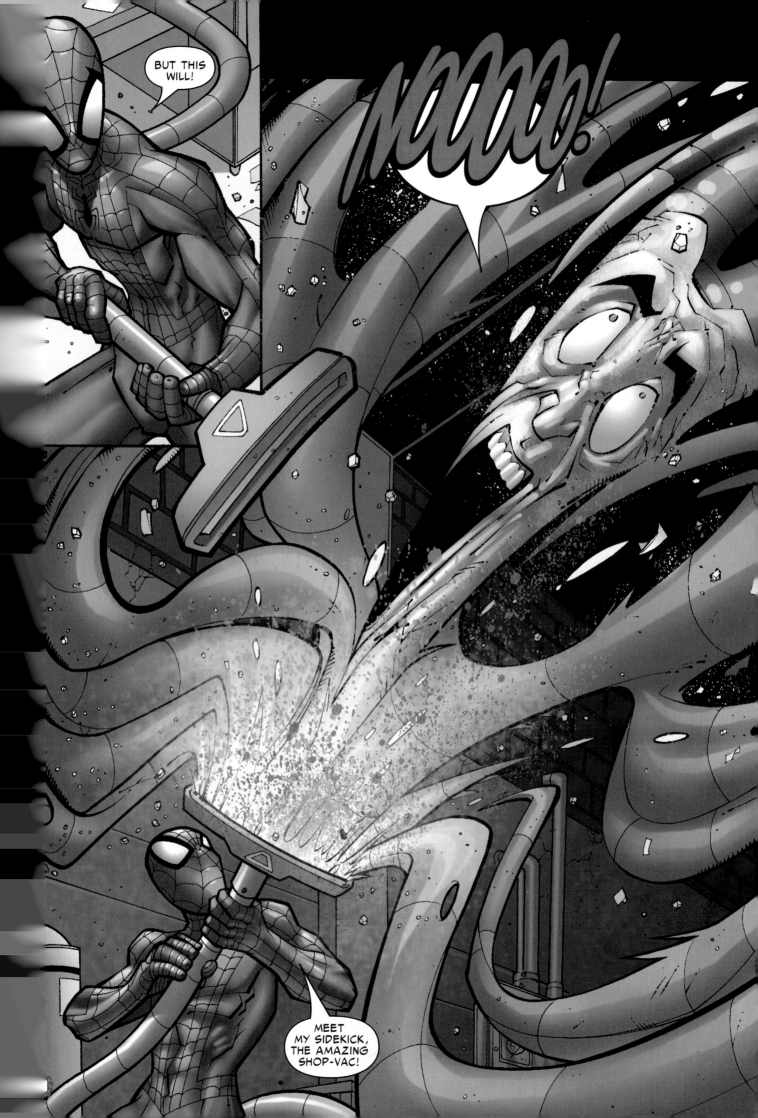

I'M FREE!
OH BOY, HERE WE GO AGAIN...
WHAT THE HECK?!
THUMP!
THUMP!
THUMP!
THUMP!

ANSWERS!

Take a look below and see how well you did! Remember though, no peeking before you've answered all the puzzles, guys!

SPIDEY'S WEB OF PUZZLES!

SUPER VILLAIN SHOWDOWN!

N	M	O	R	T	C	E	L	E	T	A
Q	U	Y	A	R	M	Y	S	T	E	R	I	O
A	K	E	R	V	B	G	T	M	G	I	V	V
R	E	E	I	M	A	K	R	R	H	I	N	O
N	K	L	Z	O	S	A	C	B	C	I	K
A	C	R	D	I	P	A	E	O	L	E	I	V
G	A	B	A	F	E	O	M	B	L	J	I	U
F	E	U	D	T	L	B	O	D	O	R	G	L
A	L	J	C	K	E	G	A	O	M	O	P	T
A	U	S	I	S	B	N	N	U	S	A	I	U
J	A	C	K	S	L	A	N	T	E	R	N	R
U	A	S	H	O	C	K	E	R	E	R	N	U
			R	G	E	E		

A STING IN THE TALE!

LUKE CAGE

SPIDER-MAN

DAREDEVIL

SPIDER-WOMAN

SAY WHAT?

A=2, B=5, C-1, D=3, E=4

MULTIPLE MENACE!

Clone D is the identical match

TENTACLED TERROR!

Tentacle C is holding the bomb

THESE ARE THE COUNTERS FOR THE WICKED BOARD GAME ON PAGE 34!

YOU CAN PHOTOCOPY THIS PAGE IF YOU DON'T WANT TO CUT THEM OUT!

62